Messrs.
MOONY, WORMTAIL, PADFOOT & PRONGS
are proud to present

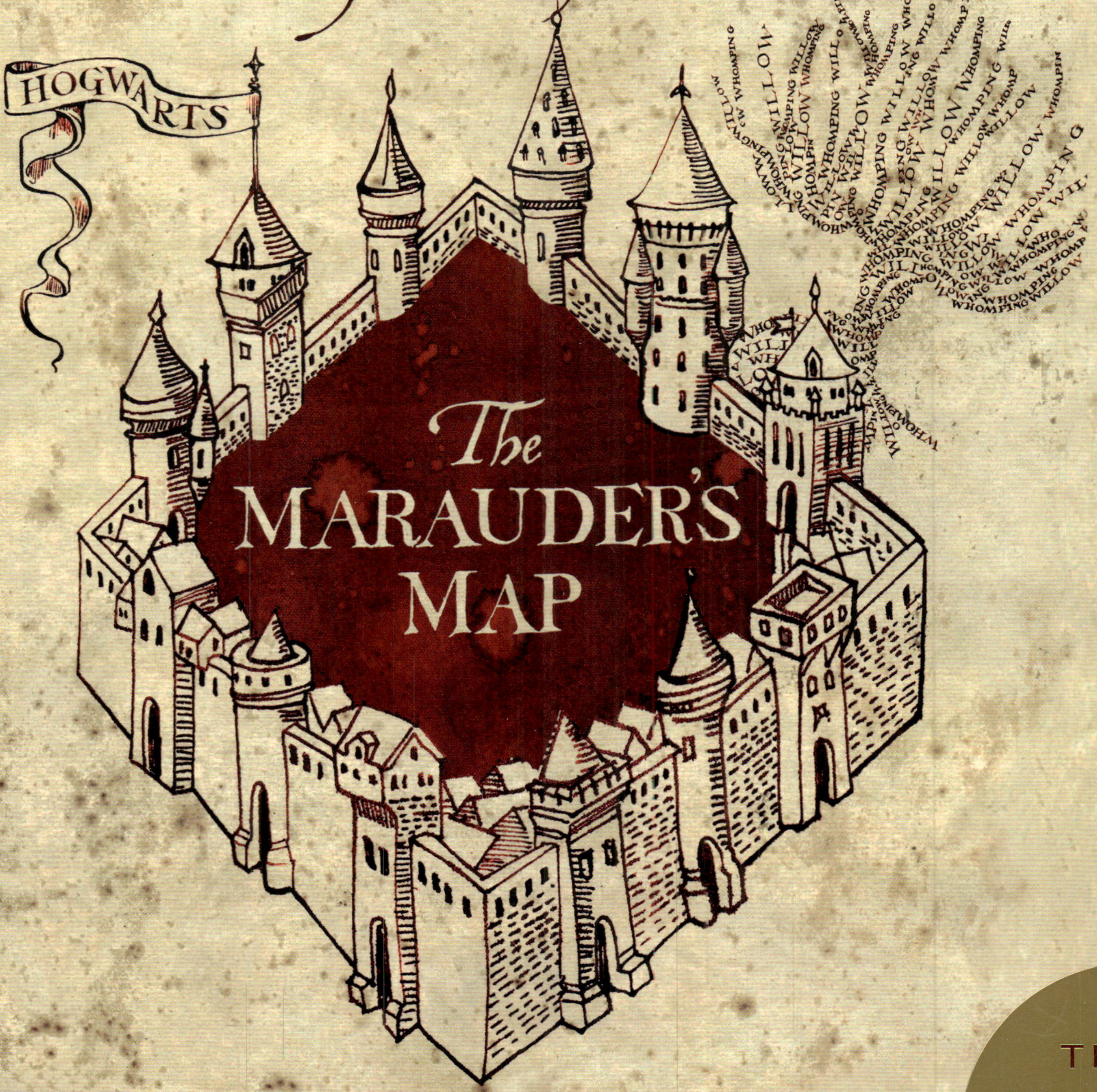

TRACK SCHEDULES OF 6 FAMILY MEMBERS!

Harry Potter
HOGWARTS™
FAMILY WALL PLANNER
2026

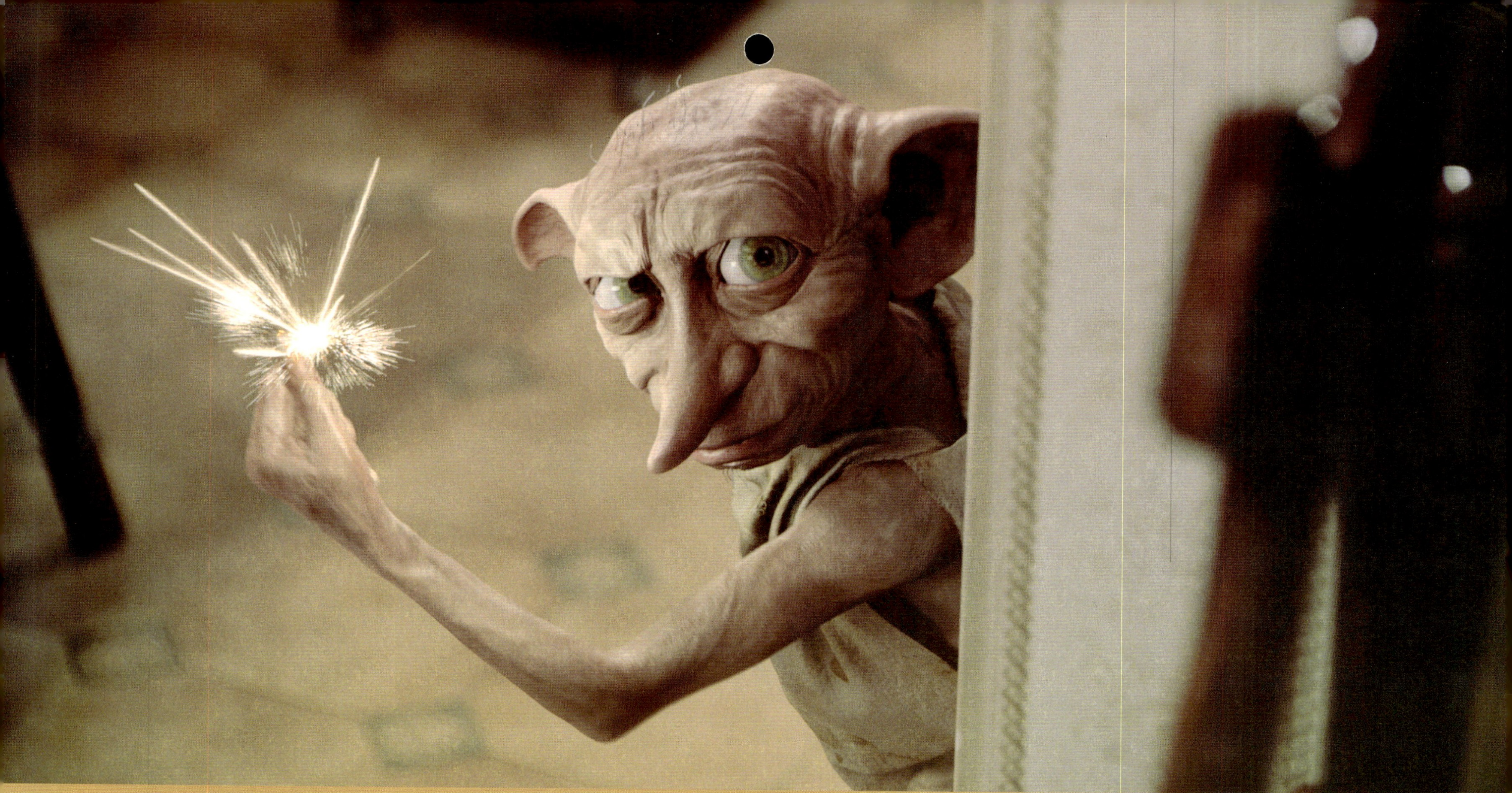

JANUARY

2026						
1 THURSDAY New Year's Day						
2 FRIDAY						
3 SATURDAY						
4 SUNDAY						
5 MONDAY						
6 TUESDAY						
7 WEDNESDAY						
8 THURSDAY						
9 FRIDAY						
10 SATURDAY						

12 MONDAY						
13 TUESDAY						
14 WEDNESDAY						
15 THURSDAY						
16 FRIDAY						
17 SATURDAY						
18 SUNDAY						
19 MONDAY Martin Luther King Jr. Day						
20 TUESDAY						
21 WEDNESDAY						
22 THURSDAY						
23 FRIDAY						
24 SATURDAY						
25 SUNDAY						
26 MONDAY						
27 TUESDAY						
28 WEDNESDAY						
29 THURSDAY						
30 FRIDAY						
31 SATURDAY						

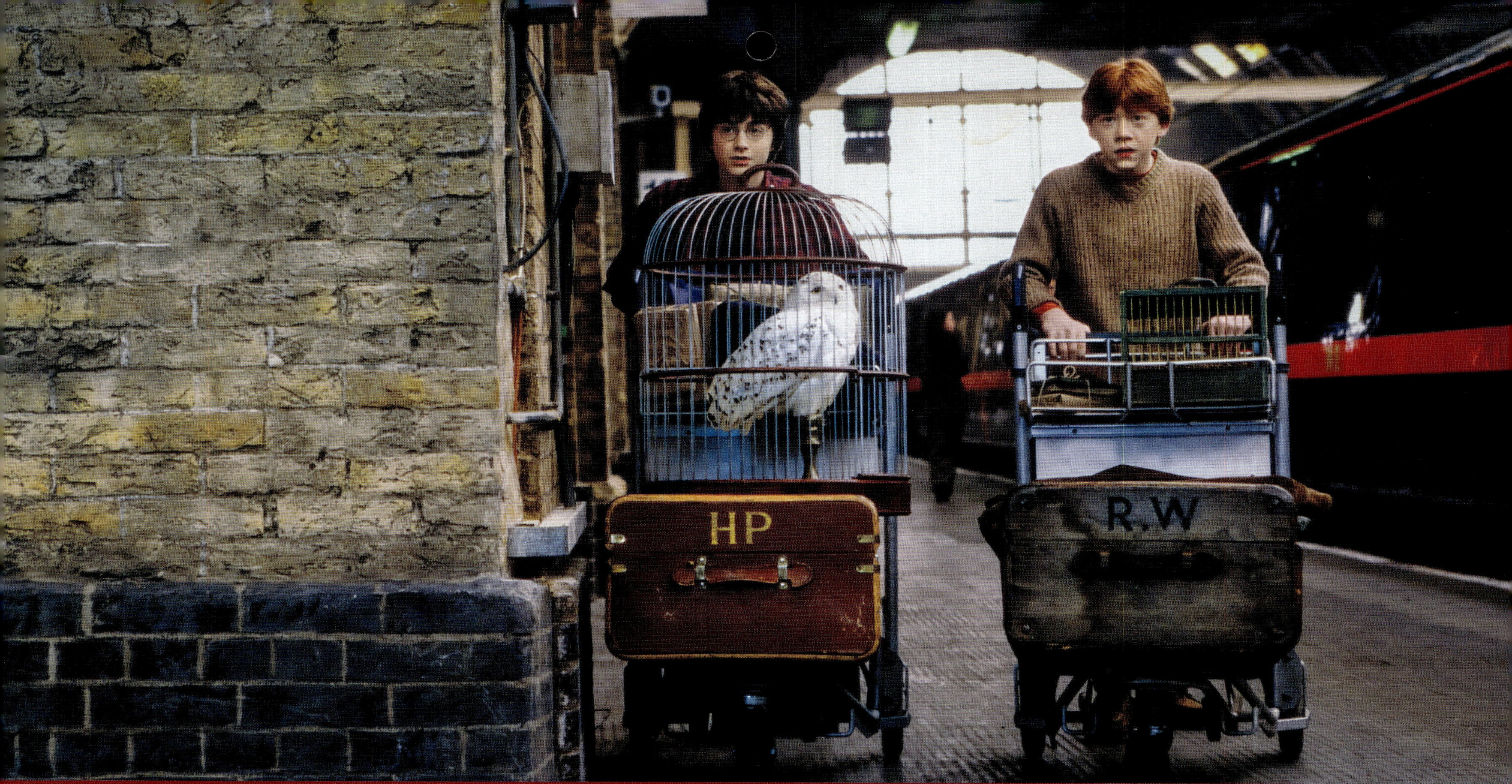

FEBRUARY

2026						
1 SUNDAY						
2 MONDAY Groundhog Day						
3 TUESDAY						
4 WEDNESDAY						
5 THURSDAY						
6 FRIDAY						
7 SATURDAY						
8 SUNDAY						
9 MONDAY						

12 THURSDAY

13 FRIDAY

14 SATURDAY
Valentine's Day

15 SUNDAY

16 MONDAY
Presidents Day
Washington's Birthday

17 TUESDAY

18 WEDNESDAY

19 THURSDAY

20 FRIDAY

21 SATURDAY

22 SUNDAY

23 MONDAY

24 TUESDAY

25 WEDNESDAY

26 THURSDAY

27 FRIDAY

28 SATURDAY

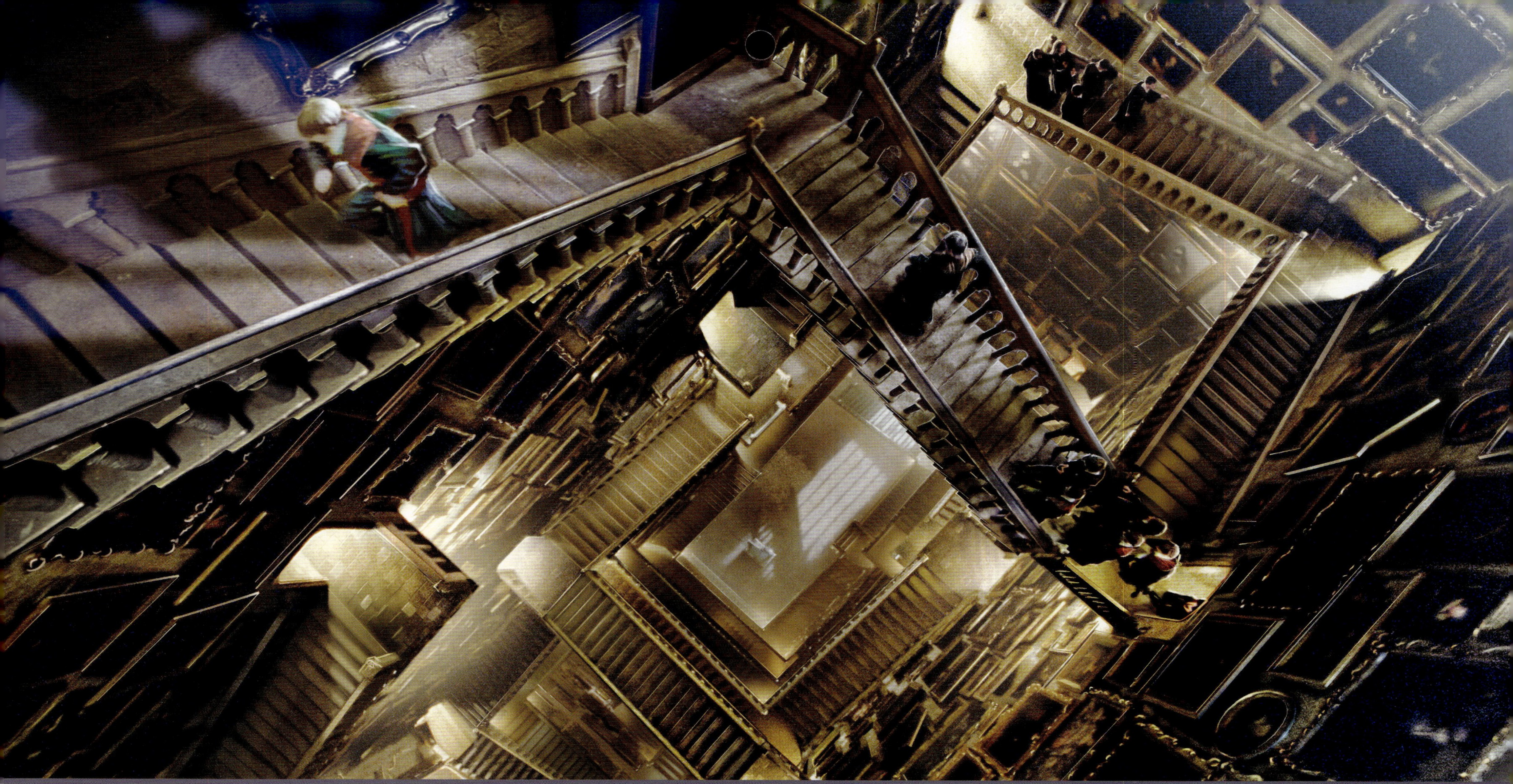

MARCH

2026						
1 SUNDAY Ron Weasley's Birthday						
2 MONDAY						
3 TUESDAY						
4 WEDNESDAY						
5 THURSDAY						
6 FRIDAY						
7 SATURDAY						
8 SUNDAY Daylight Saving Time Begins						
9 MONDAY						

11 WEDNESDAY						
12 THURSDAY						
13 FRIDAY						
14 SATURDAY						
15 SUNDAY						
16 MONDAY						
17 TUESDAY Saint Patrick's Day						
18 WEDNESDAY						
19 THURSDAY						
20 FRIDAY						
21 SATURDAY						
22 SUNDAY						
23 MONDAY						
24 TUESDAY						
25 WEDNESDAY						
26 THURSDAY						
27 FRIDAY						
28 SATURDAY						
29 SUNDAY						
30 MONDAY						
31 TUESDAY						

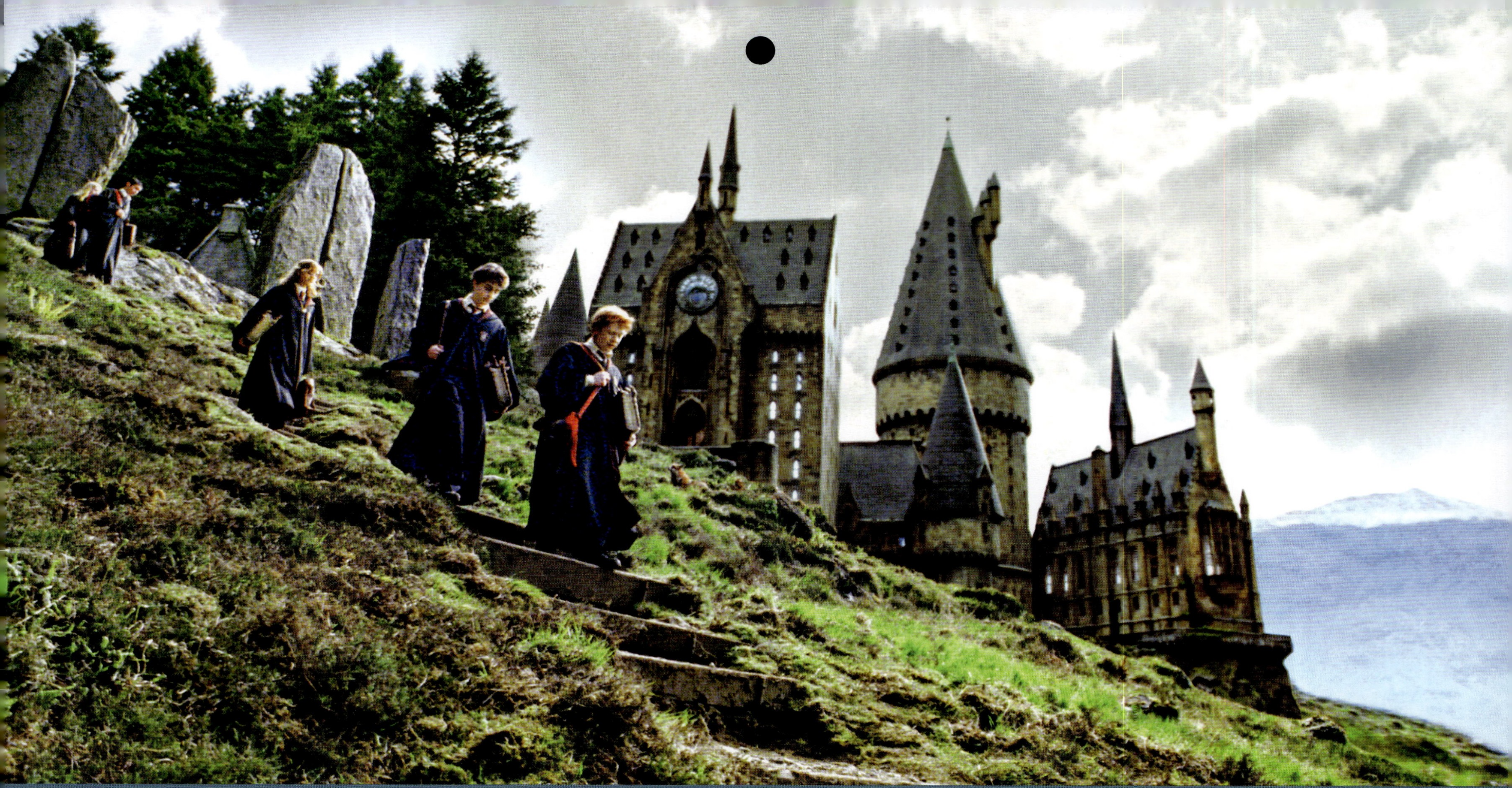

APRIL

2026						
1 WEDNESDAY April Fools' Day First Day of Passover						
2 THURSDAY						
3 FRIDAY Good Friday						
4 SATURDAY						
5 SUNDAY Easter						
6 MONDAY						
7 TUESDAY						
8 WEDNESDAY						
9 THURSDAY						

11 SATURDAY						
12 SUNDAY						
13 MONDAY						
14 TUESDAY						
15 WEDNESDAY						
16 THURSDAY						
17 FRIDAY						
18 SATURDAY						
19 SUNDAY						
20 MONDAY						
21 TUESDAY						
22 WEDNESDAY Earth Day						
23 THURSDAY						
24 FRIDAY						
25 SATURDAY						
26 SUNDAY						
27 MONDAY						
28 TUESDAY						
29 WEDNESDAY						
30 THURSDAY						

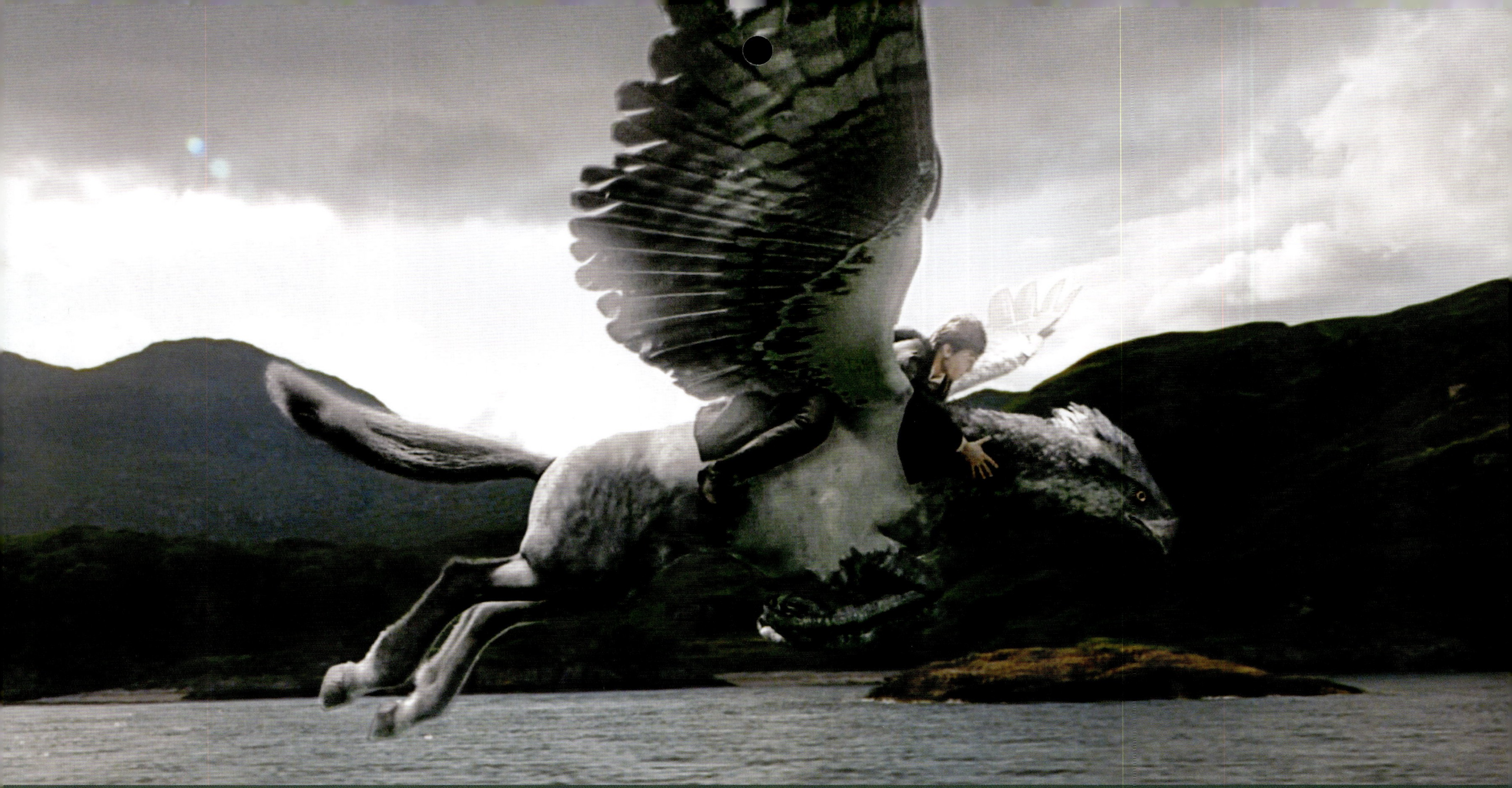

MAY

2026						
1 FRIDAY						
2 SATURDAY Anniversary of the Battle of Hogwarts						
3 SUNDAY						
4 MONDAY Early May Bank Holiday (UK)						
5 TUESDAY						
6 WEDNESDAY						
7 THURSDAY						
8 FRIDAY						
9 SATURDAY						
10 SUNDAY						

12 TUESDAY						
13 WEDNESDAY						
14 THURSDAY						
15 FRIDAY						
16 SATURDAY						
17 SUNDAY						
18 MONDAY						
19 TUESDAY						
20 WEDNESDAY						
21 THURSDAY						
22 FRIDAY						
23 SATURDAY						
24 SUNDAY						
25 MONDAY Memorial Day Spring Bank Holiday (UK)						
26 TUESDAY						
27 WEDNSEDAY						
28 THURSDAY						
29 FRIDAY						
30 SATURDAY						
31 SUNDAY						

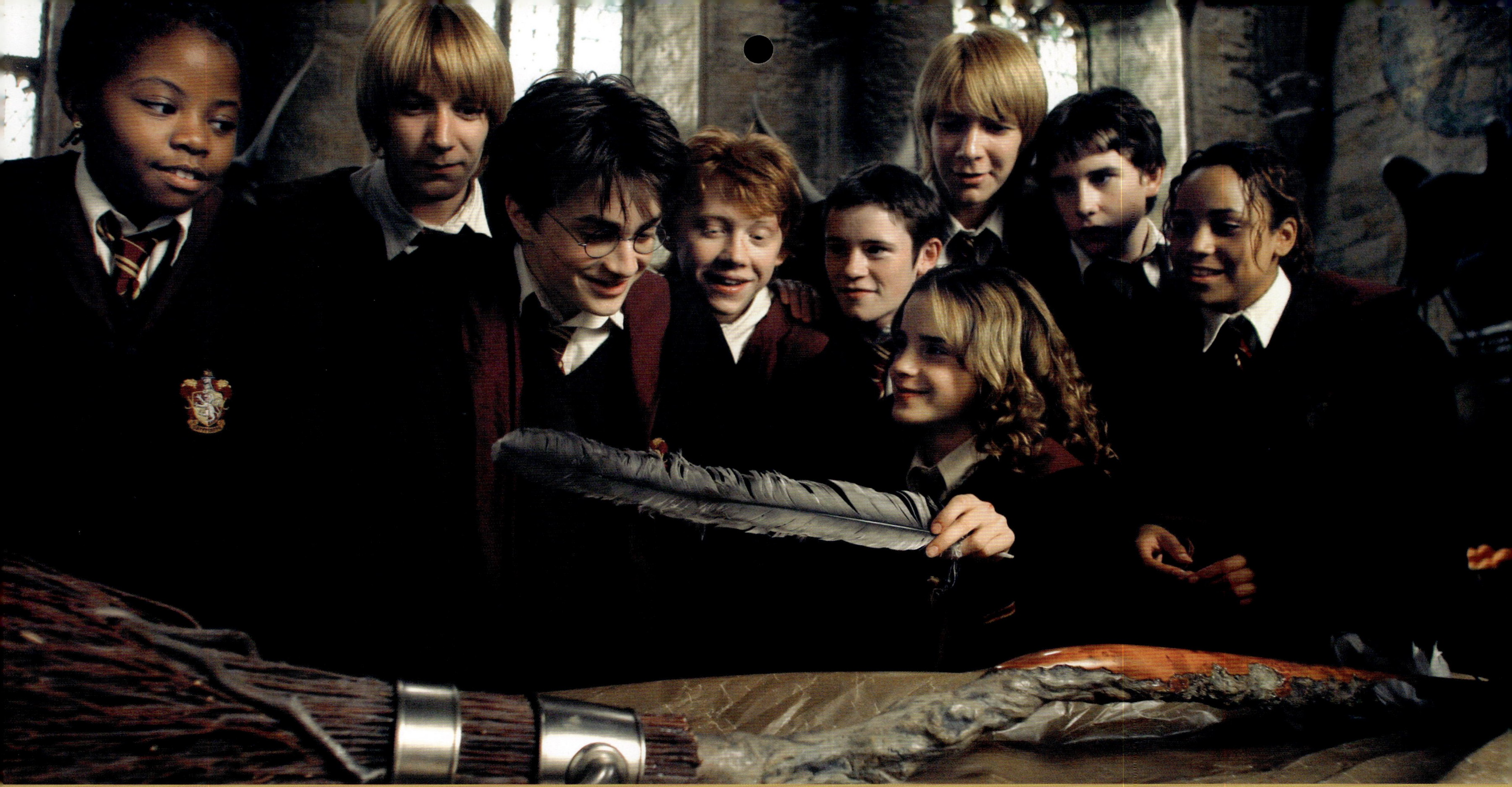

JUNE

2026						
1 MONDAY						
2 TUESDAY						
3 WEDNESDAY						
4 THURSDAY						
5 FRIDAY						
6 SATURDAY						
7 SUNDAY						
8 MONDAY						
9 TUESDAY						

11 THURSDAY						
12 FRIDAY						
13 SATURDAY						
14 SUNDAY						
15 MONDAY						
16 TUESDAY						
17 WEDNESDAY						
18 THURSDAY						
19 FRIDAY Juneteenth						
20 SATURDAY						
21 SUNDAY Father's Day						
22 MONDAY						
23 TUESDAY						
24 WEDNESDAY						
25 THURSDAY						
26 FRIDAY						
27 SATURDAY						
28 SUNDAY						
29 MONDAY						
30 TUESDAY						

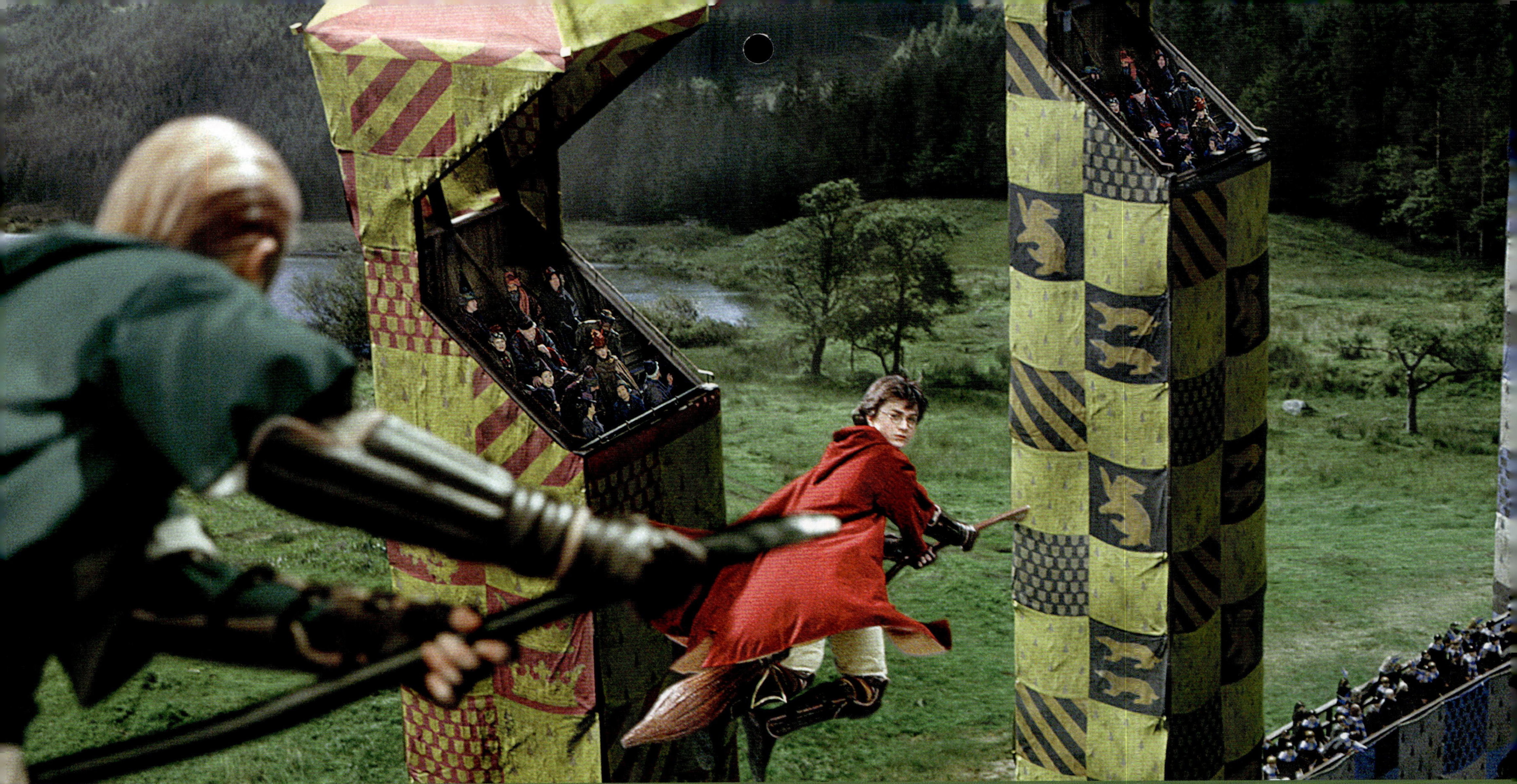

JULY

2026						
1 WEDNESDAY						
2 THURSDAY						
3 FRIDAY						
4 SATURDAY Independence Day						
5 SUNDAY						
6 MONDAY						
7 TUESDAY						
8 WEDNESDAY						
9 THURSDAY						

11 SATURDAY						
12 SUNDAY						
13 MONDAY						
14 TUESDAY						
15 WEDNESDAY						
16 THURSDAY						
17 FRIDAY						
18 SATURDAY						
19 SUNDAY						
20 MONDAY						
21 TUESDAY						
22 WEDNESDAY						
23 THURSDAY						
24 FRIDAY						
25 SATURDAY						
26 SUNDAY						
27 MONDAY						
28 TUESDAY						
29 WEDNESDAY						
30 THURSDAY						
31 FRIDAY Harry Potter's Birthday						

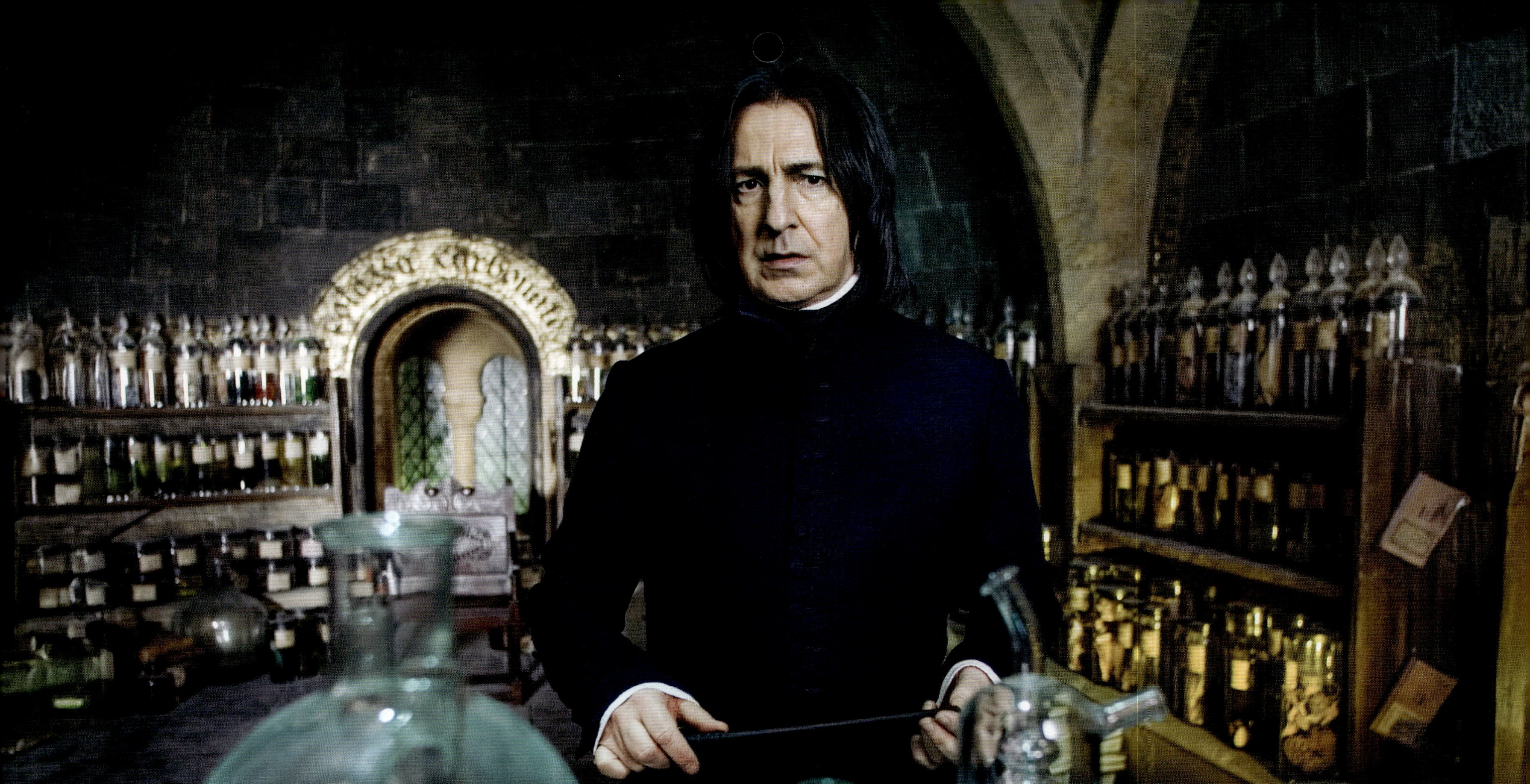

AUGUST

2026						
1 SATURDAY						
2 SUNDAY						
3 MONDAY						
4 TUESDAY						
5 WEDNESDAY						
6 THURSDAY						
7 FRIDAY						
8 SATURDAY						
9 SUNDAY						
10 MONDAY						

11 TUESDAY						
12 WEDNESDAY						
13 THURSDAY						
14 FRIDAY						
15 SATURDAY						
16 SUNDAY						
17 MONDAY						
18 TUESDAY						
19 WEDNESDAY						
20 THURSDAY						
21 FRIDAY						
22 SATURDAY						
23 SUNDAY						
24 MONDAY						
25 TUESDAY						
26 WEDNESDAY						
27 THURSDAY						
28 FRIDAY						
29 SATURDAY						
30 SUNDAY						
31 MONDAY Summer Bank Holiday (UK)						

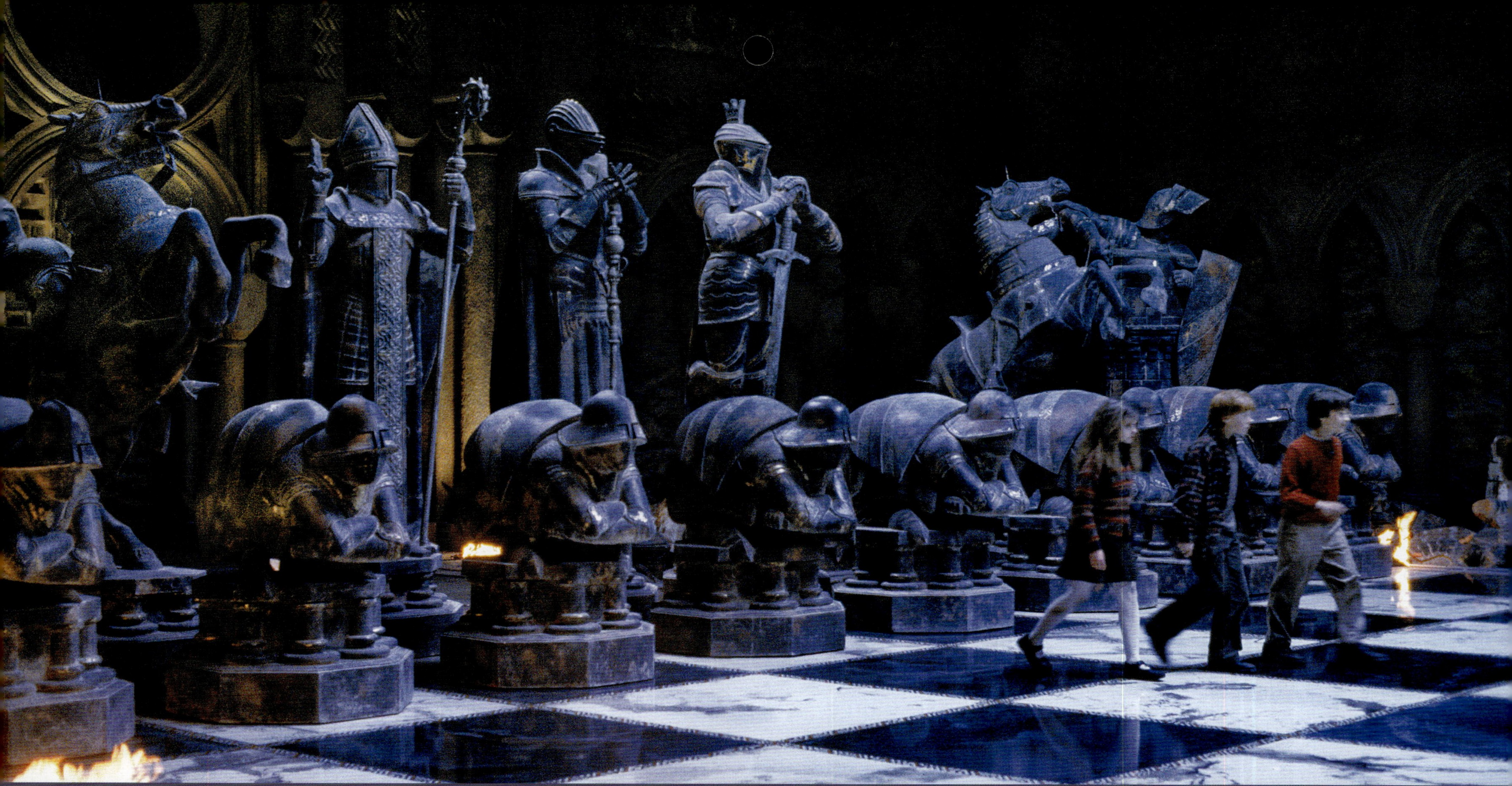

SEPTEMBER

2026						
1 TUESDAY						
2 WEDNESDAY						
3 THURSDAY						
4 FRIDAY						
5 SATURDAY						
6 SUNDAY						
7 MONDAY Labor Day						
8 TUESDAY						
9 WEDNESDAY						
10 THURSDAY						

Begins at Sundown						
12 SATURDAY						
13 SUNDAY						
14 MONDAY						
15 TUESDAY						
16 WEDNESDAY						
17 THURSDAY						
18 FRIDAY						
19 SATURDAY Hermione Granger's Birthday						
20 SUNDAY Yom Kippur Begins at Sundown						
21 MONDAY						
22 TUESDAY						
23 WEDNESDAY						
24 THURSDAY						
25 FRIDAY						
26 SATURDAY						
27 SUNDAY						
28 MONDAY						
29 TUESDAY						
30 WEDNESDAY						

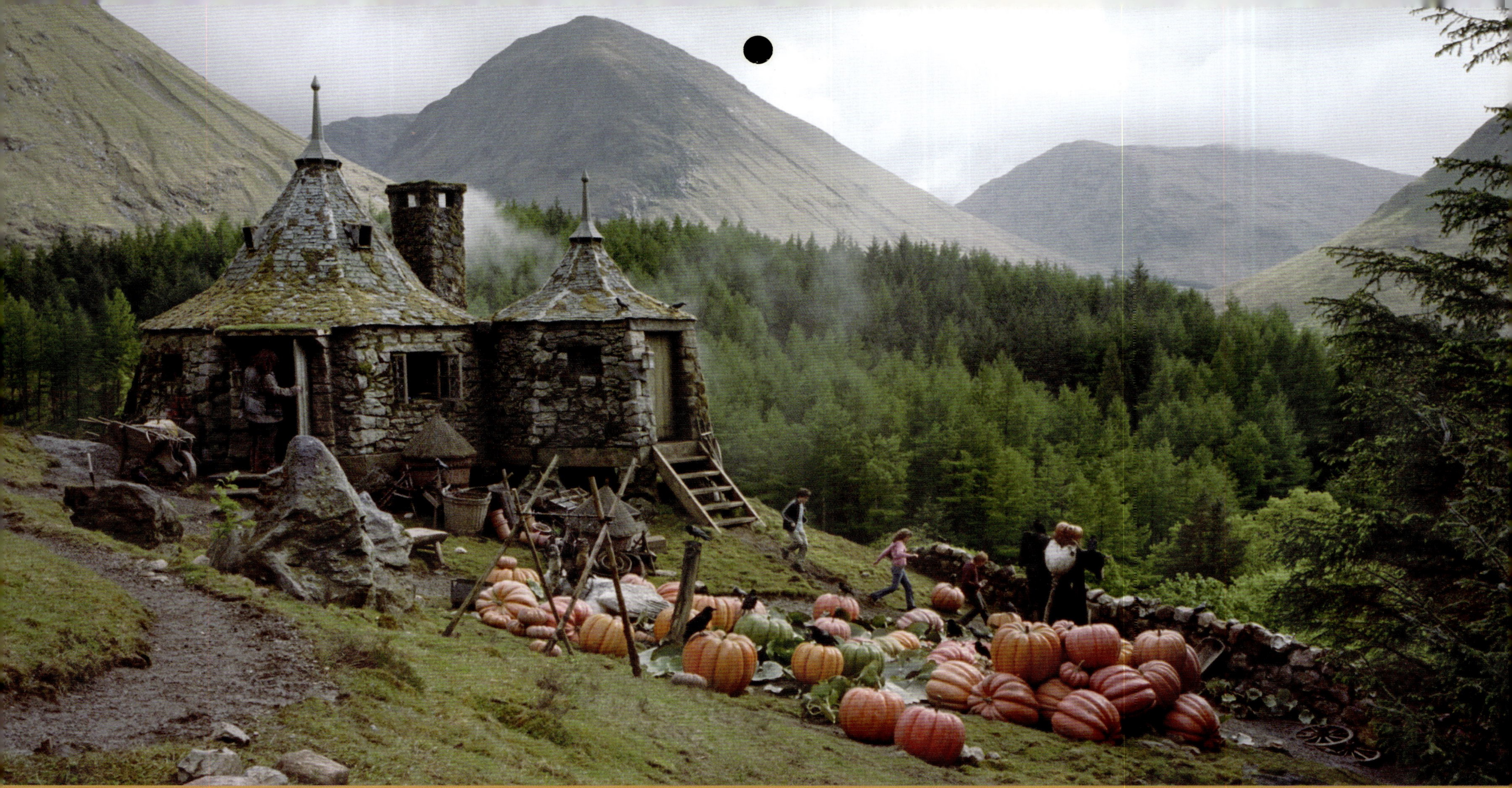

OCTOBER

2026						
1 THURSDAY						
2 FRIDAY						
3 SATURDAY						
4 SUNDAY						
5 MONDAY						
6 TUESDAY						
7 WEDNESDAY						
8 THURSDAY						
9 FRIDAY						

12 MONDAY Columbus Day Indigenous Peoples' Day						
13 TUESDAY						
14 WEDNESDAY						
15 THURSDAY						
16 FRIDAY						
17 SATURDAY						
18 SUNDAY						
19 MONDAY						
20 TUESDAY						
21 WEDNESDAY						
22 THURSDAY						
23 FRIDAY						
24 SATURDAY						
25 SUNDAY						
26 MONDAY						
27 TUESDAY						
28 WEDNESDAY						
29 THURSDAY						
30 FRIDAY						
31 SATURDAY Halloween						

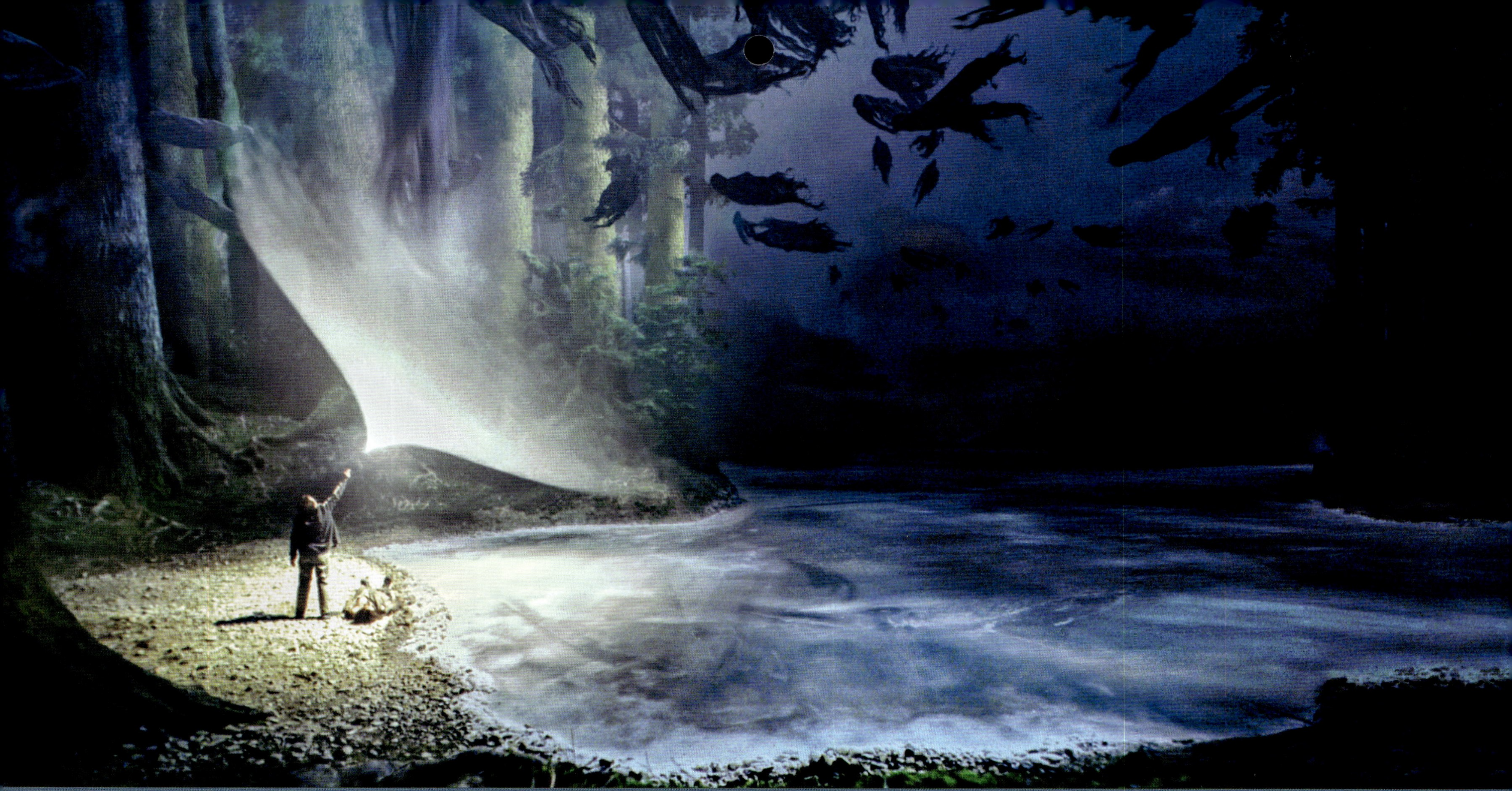

NOVEMBER

2026							
1 SUNDAY Daylight Saving Time Ends							
2 MONDAY							
3 TUESDAY Election Day							
4 WEDNESDAY							
5 THURSDAY							
6 FRIDAY							
7 SATURDAY							
8 SUNDAY							
9 MONDAY							

Veterans Day						
12 THURSDAY						
13 FRIDAY						
14 SATURDAY						
15 SUNDAY						
16 MONDAY						
17 TUESDAY						
18 WEDNESDAY						
19 THURSDAY						
20 FRIDAY						
21 SATURDAY						
22 SUNDAY						
23 MONDAY						
24 TUESDAY						
25 WEDNESDAY						
26 THURSDAY Thanksgiving						
27 FRIDAY						
28 SATURDAY						
29 SUNDAY						
30 MONDAY						

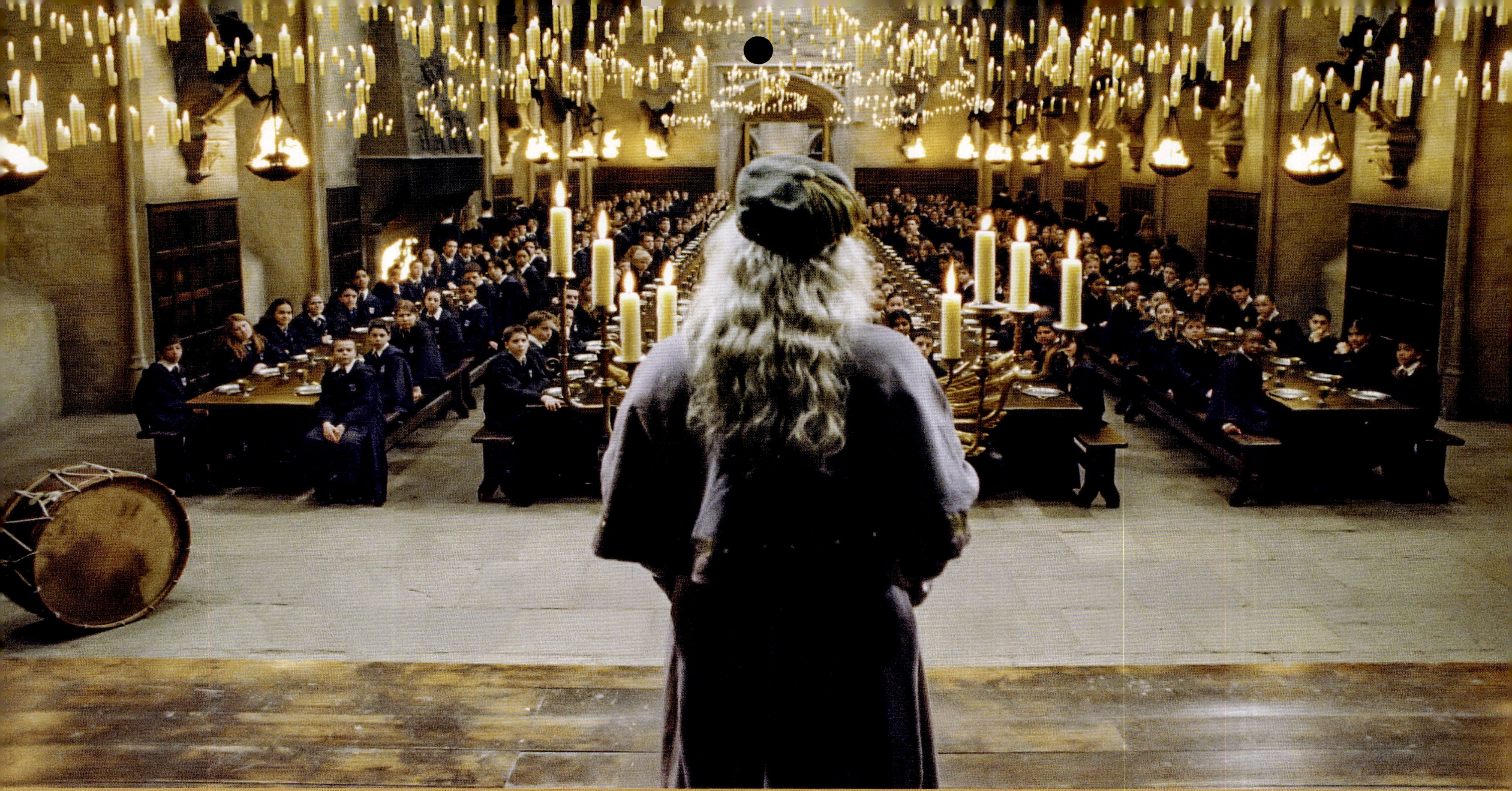

DECEMBER

2026						
1 TUESDAY						
2 WEDNESDAY						
3 THURSDAY						
4 FRIDAY Hanukkah Begins at Sundown						
5 SATURDAY						
6 SUNDAY						
7 MONDAY						
8 TUESDAY						
9 WEDNESDAY						

12 SATURDAY						
13 SUNDAY						
14 MONDAY						
15 TUESDAY						
16 WEDNESDAY						
17 THURSDAY						
18 FRIDAY						
19 SATURDAY						
20 SUNDAY						
21 MONDAY						
22 TUESDAY						
23 WEDNESDAY						
24 THURSDAY Christmas Eve						
25 FRIDAY Christmas Day						
26 SATURDAY First Day of Kwanzaa Boxing Day						
27 SUNDAY						
28 MONDAY						
29 TUESDAY						
30 WEDNESDAY						
31 THURSDAY New Year's Eve						

Harry Potter

HOGWARTS™ 2026 12-Month Family Wall Planner

KEEP TRACK OF YOUR FAMILY'S BUSY SCHEDULE with this 2026 Hogwarts™-inspired 12-month wall planner. This vertical-format wall planner offers space to record the comings and goings of up to six different family members in this unique month-at-a-glance grid format. Included are three large sticker sheets of planner and decorative stickers to customize the calendar days with your to-dos and events, and write-in name stickers for each family member to pick which Hogwarts™ icon they want to be represented by each month.

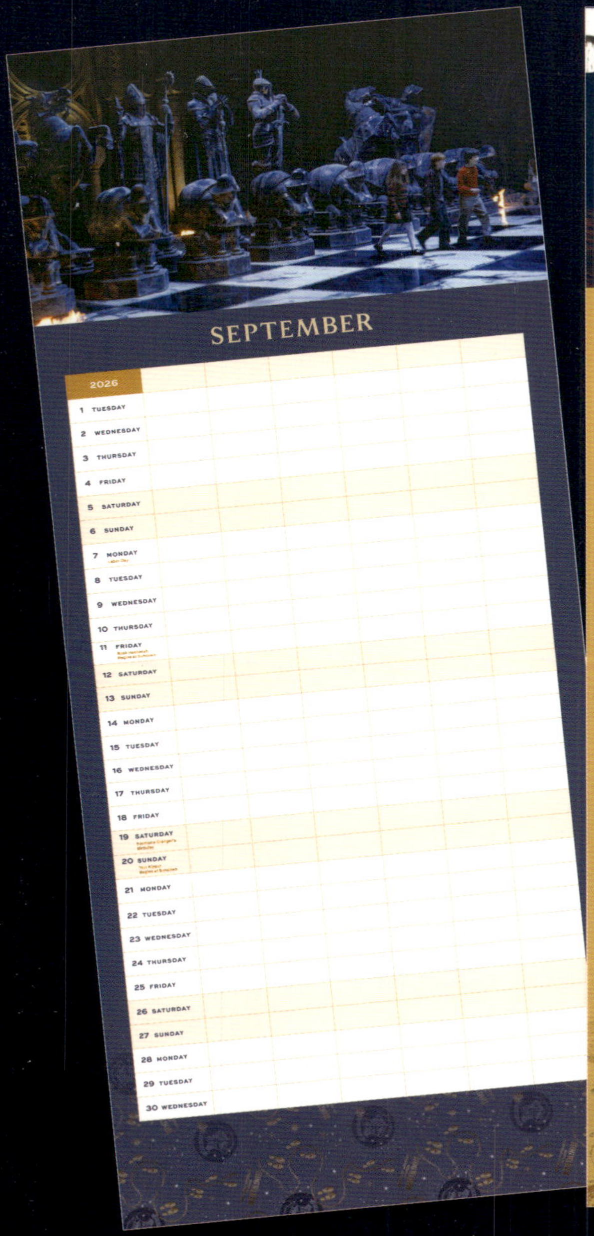

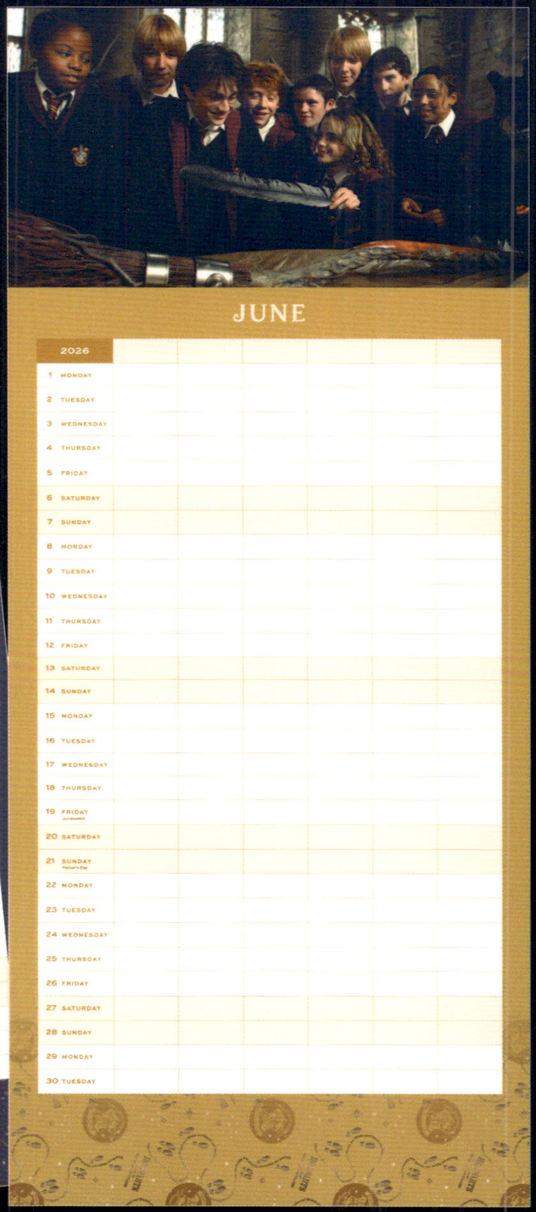

12-MONTH VERTICAL ORGANIZER!

- Room for 6 family schedules
- 3 Big sheets of planner stickers
- Storage pocket

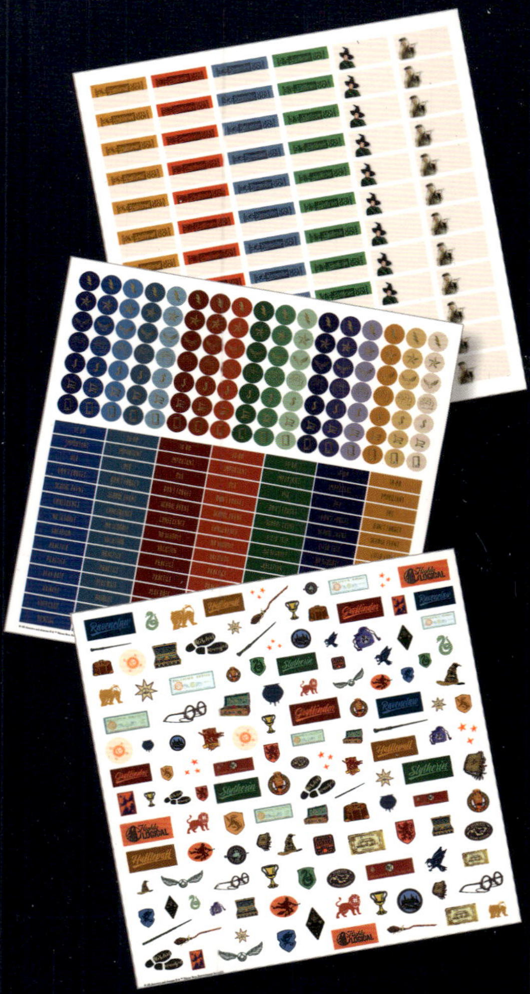

Insight Editions, in association with Roots of Peace, will plant two trees for each tree used in the manufacturing of Insights products.

MIX Paper from responsible sources FSC® C112006

INSIGHT EDITIONS
insighteditions.com

ISBN: 979-8-3374-0047-1
$16.99 US / $22.99 CAN

MANUFACTURED IN CHINA